Let Him Kiss Me

Lacresha Hayes

Lanico Media House
Celebrating literary lessons and legacies
TEXAS • ARKANSAS • LOUISIANA

Copyright ©2016 Lacresha Hayes
All rights reserved.

No portion of this book may be reproduced in any form, mechanical, digital or otherwise without written permission from the author.

ISBN: 978-0-9967799-8-2

Lanico Media House
Printed in the United States.

Check out these Kindle exclusives by Lacresha Hayes:

The Path to Oneness

The Ultimate Survival Guide for the Entrepreneurial Woman

Tangled

Full length books:

The Rape of Innocence
Becoming: My Personal Memoirs
Raw Redemption
Poetic Infinity
Truth and Intimacy
Heart Strings
A Heart in Motion
Earmageddon
Adjacent Smiles
Cascade of Tears
Unnecessary Roughness
The Snare of a Strange Woman

For my family. I love to write but it is your continued support and love for me that motivates me to keep going forward.

Lacresha Hayes

Acknowledgments

The deeper love goes, the more difficult it is to find words for it. Gratitude is much the same way. In fact, words have been so often manipulated that when it comes to capturing true bonds, true emotions, no words ever measure up. But how can I not try just the same?

I have to acknowledge the man who taught me that love and ownership has not a thing to do with one another. He taught me that romance does not have to be physical, that distance doesn't stop a touch and presence has nothing to do with physicality. This same man taught me that I can hold on as long as I want or let go whenever I want without explaining myself to anyone. He inspired me to finally write about the side of me I would rather have kept private. He encouraged me not to be ashamed of being a woman, having needs, wishes, desires and sexuality. Finally, he helped me answer the age old question: is there really a such thing as love at first sight. The answer was a resounding yes!

James R. Davis, Sr. is probably one of the most dynamic men I've ever met, self-possessed, powerful, tempered, focused, driven, inspirational and faith-filled. He is also one of my best friends, my mentor, and my occasional butt-kicker. Without him, I would have never written a book like this, and certainly, I would not have published it. To him I simply say, long live the king!

Let Him Kiss Me

I must also acknowledge my editor who worked with me to put this book together, Ashley Smith. She has this eye for detail that is truly invaluable.

A big huge thank you to all the influencers who have helped to make the release of this book a huge deal.

Introduction

When I first started writing this book, I wasn't sure it would actually be a book. I knew that my relationship coaching was taking off and a lot of people wanted to hear real talk about real life relationships. Many wanted a book that would walk them through real situations. Truth is, all relationships go through phases. So eventually, this book took shape out of my own love stories and those I heard about or witnessed.

This book is composed of poetry, journal or diary entries, letters to the spouse. It is a very passionate composition of love, trust, loss, grief, faith and resurrection. There is something in here for every relationship at any stage. Further, there are tons of portions that will inspire you and your mate to reach a deeper level of intimacy.

Now for the disclaimer. This book is sexual and intimate because real relationships are sexual and intimate or at the very least they should be. There are a lot of steamy scenes. If you read them and allow them, they will create or recreate a fire inside you for your spouse, which is the purpose of them. Remember, this is your spouse. This is what sex was made for, for you and your mate to not only procreate, but also to enjoy one another, to pleasure one another, to bond on a deeper level than any other bond between people.

With that being said, let's hop right into this beautiful journey called *Let Him Kiss Me*. Umm. Have fun!

Lacresha Hayes

We Meet

Just Once

My mother leaned over and whispered,
"Open your eyes."
But if I open my eyes
Reality will come crashing in
Cause there just ain't no way
I've finally found my just once

You know, just once can you really give your heart
Just once to feel
Just once to heal
Just once to dream
Just once to touch
To taste
To see
To hear
To smell
The truth and power of love

I squeeze my eyes tighter
My mother begs me to open them
She doesn't understand
She cannot know
That I'm holding on to my just once

Today

He looked at me today.
He focused in
From my head to my toes
Slowly he scanned every inch of me
And genuinely looked at me today.

He hugged me today.
I mean really, he hugged me.
He wrapped both arms around me
And with every muscle in his body
He hugged me today.

He kissed me today.
With both lips
With teeth and tongue
And with a fire that ignited my heart
He kissed me today.

But he loves me every day.
Though each day brings a different way
Yet, each one he chooses to stay
And though his attention may sway
He loves me every day.

Just Do

You asked me why?
I just do.
Do I need a reason
To be in love with you?

I didn't expect it, honey.
Ooh, the love that I feel!
My soul is happy,
I am starting to heal.

I can blame the peace in your presence,
Or maybe the passion in your voice.
Possibly the care in your caress,
Whatever it may be, you are my choice.

You keep questioning,
You want to know why?
I just do.
And will until I die.

Lacresha Hayes

My Hope is Screaming

We sat on the couch
We watched some TV
We did a little hugging
We did a lot of laughing
We did some talking
A little bit of noticing
Stolen glances with new eyes
And I feel you again
Moving around inside me
And it feels really good
Something so familiar
Bittersweet though
Because the fall from here is great
I know the sting of disappointment
But my hope is screaming
And I feel such joy
My hope is singing
Why silence her?

Let Him Kiss Me

Key Lime Pie

You know how much I love it
But you want some of it
And to me, it is so precious
My hidden treasure
But you want some of it

It took time to construct this pie
The ingredients were all natural
Then I had to let it chill
Let the flavors meld
The whole while looking forward to it
And now all of a sudden, you want some of it

You say, "Baby, I know that stuff gotta be good!"
I respond, "Oh, I know it is!"
See, I've been carefully crafting this thing
Until I got it just so
You keep looking at me with that look in your eyes
I keep telling you to be patient
If there is anything worth waiting for
It's my key lime pie.

Lacresha Hayes

A Reason To Wait

Everyone is naked
Every butt is big
The hair is long and wavy
The makeup no longer comes off
Every woman is twerking
A lot of men still paying
Sex is like french fries, fast and everywhere
You don't have to wait on it
You asked me why you should wait
When you can decorate your plate
With a variety, each as exotic as the other
But none of them are me
They cannot give what I can
Cannot love like I love
Will not stay like I will
Cannot endure what I've endured
They will share their bodies
But their hearts are fragmented
They will bring you fun
But they cannot walk with you into freedom
They can give you what you want
But none can be the woman you need
If you need a reason to wait
Do it because you deserve more

Let Him Kiss Me

To Comfort You

You wanted to quit your job today
Times has been so hard
Death in the family
Bills always due
Work that needs to be done
But there is never any time for you

You need to go outside and mow the lawn
But you'd rather grab a beer and a blunt
You keep trying to relax your mind, but it is fixed on your fears
People who want what you have
They keep coming and calling, asking you to do
Then I walk in after my own long day wanting some time and attention too

The pressures of a man are unfathomable
You take the world to rest on your shoulders
Seems the more you care, the more it hurts
Cause some are only here to take from you
Some present for validation
But I, my darling, am here to comfort you

Lacresha Hayes

You Entered Me

I was in the middle of my errands
I had so much stuff to do
I didn't really have time
To be fantasizing about you

My phone rang
Somehow I knew it was you
You've been calling a lot more
You want me stuck to you like glue

I listened to your voice
My soul was filled with the sound
I felt your presence with me
Though you were nowhere around

You have entered me
Our souls are united
Into my heart, my mind, my life
You are invited

Let Him Kiss Me

Prep Time

I've awaited his arrival since the time that he left.

I've showered, shaved, shampooed and perfumed.

The bed is full of clothes but nothing fits just right.

For you, my love, it has to be tight.

Eyelashes, lipstick, eyeliner, lotions
Nail polish, powders, and matching jewelry
Every hair has to be in place
I can't wait to see that look on your face

Finally, you're home and my day is made
I'm on the bed in a provocative way
But I jump up and decide to meet you at the door

As I thought, your jaw hits the floor

It gives me great pleasure to make you smile
I adore the way you look at me
You grabbed me and gave me a long kiss
It's days like this I never again want to miss

I Surrender

I had never really been kissed
So many opportunities missed
Never really been hugged
Never had my heart tugged

I have never fell in so deep
Never met a man I truly wanted to keep
Had never felt hands so strong
Had never been caressed so long

I had never looked out the window so much
Awaiting your arrival and your touch
Tonight we're going all the way
I won't leave anymore. I want to stay

It's like you know when you look in my eyes
My surrender comes as no surprise
You ravished me and set my heart free
As our bodies meld and our souls agree

First Night's Musings

I can feel your breath on my neck and face. You're holding me so tightly as you sleep the sleep of satisfaction. You're slightly snoring but it doesn't bother me at all. I like the sound and find it rather comforting.

I'm tired but cannot sleep. I keep touching you, smelling you and looking at you. I try to move away a little so that I can take more of you in, but you lock in tighter and mumble something with the word "mine" in it. I smile even as a tear comes to my eyes. And now I know for sure, you love me. But more importantly, sweetheart, I love you.

Daydreaming

I woke up smiling. You texted me to see how I was doing. I was still lying in the same spot you left me. Ha! I wondered whether I should tell you that, but you probably wouldn't believe me.

We texted back and forth a couple of times and I laid back down in the same spot.

Daydreaming.

Happy.

Content for a change.

I exhaled, and sleep found me once more. And it should come as no surprise that I dreamed of you.

Let Him Kiss Me

I Come

This heat is too much
Like an eternal flame
Burning ever stronger
Intense desire
Desperate yearning
Upon my bed
My legs are spread
Sweat all over me
And this moisture does not end
It's so wet!
My face
My hair
My body shimmers
Glistening and calling
Bombs keep blasting
Volcanoes of passion erupting
Over and over
Until finally I come
Back

Lacresha Hayes

Deeper Than That

Everyone has this opinion
They keep trying to figure it out
Why him? Why her?
Is it the money? Looks? Sex?
Maybe it's magic.
They are seeking the answer
Wondering how we make it work

We fight so hard
Often we forget who the enemy is
We say things we don't mean
Mean things we can never say
Every week we try to walk away
But we come right back

You have hurt me
I have hurt you
Disappointment embittered us both
But on your worst day, I love you still
And you keep on running after me
I had asked God to break the soul tie
He simply said: "It's deeper than that."

We, honey, are deeper than that! We are destiny.

Just a Band

I started dreaming of the ring
Before I could picture the man
But the ring doesn't mean a thing
Unless the man has a plan

I had picked out a dress
Imagined my toes in the sand
But marriage becomes a mess
When the ring is just a band

So this time I want the real deal
And I'm holding out for the best
No matter how lonely I feel
I will not fail this test

Yes, I want the dream ring
Placed gingerly on my hand
I'd love to flash a little bling
But marriage is more than just a band

Lacresha Hayes

Skin You're In

I asked what most he liked seeing me in
He said, "Darling, the skin you're in."

After life has happened
You still look at it lovingly
Gazing slowly and longingly
As if there is not a mar
As if my body raises the bar
Of what nudity means to the world

Don't you see these cuts, man?
A baby came through my belly
The appendix is gone
Another cut for the gallstone
There are stretch marks for days
Unattractive in a thousand different ways
But yet your gaze remains

I said, "Baby, do you like that dress on the end?"
He said, "Not as much as the skin you're in."

He laid me down and explained some things
Touching every inch of me
To him my body was a movie
Each inch with its own story
With a desire of its own
Each part was his space to roam

He started with my toes
How they told him I care for my feet
But I'm not afraid to walk
Often have to cram them into uncomfortable positions

Let Him Kiss Me

But that in the end, I tried to keep them feeling nice

My legs, he said, told another story
Of being strong, though one had been broken
Of being different, bowed out for attention
Beautiful, flawless, though he said
As he rubbed and commented on how soft they were

My belly, he glanced, then he looked in my eyes
For there, he knew, would be tears
His hands felt warm as he caressed my belly
I closed my eyes
But he asked me to open them up
To look at myself again, but through his eyes

He leaned in and kissed my scar
That hideous scar that had bruised my heart
Crippled my mind
Burdened my soul
And then he said it,
"There was once a child…"

And I loved him then. It wasn't a superficial love.
It wasn't how handsome he is. It wasn't his intelligence. It wasn't money or ambition or anything he possessed.
It was his love, and how sweet it is.
It was how he opened me up to truly know
True love doesn't demand a show

I had been dolling and hiding and accessorizing
He had been honing in to my heart
I was dancing, entertaining, and gallivanting
He was reading my soul
I thought he loved me because he couldn't see the ugly
But he loved me because of the ugly

After all these years, we strolled the mall the other day

Lacresha Hayes

He reached down and grabbed my hand
It made me happy and I began to rattle on
Because I knew he was listening, even if he wasn't
I was all smiles as we walked by Victoria's Secret
I gave him the look and headed that way

I picked up a little blue number and a black one
"Which of these would you like to see me in?"
He looked intently but then his eyes met mine
"I love the blue. The black is tight. But all it takes to put me in the mood is to but glimpse the skin you're in."

Let Him Kiss Me

Love Maintenance

You began talking to me
I was trying to handle a little business
I wasn't really listening but I heard you speaking
You seemed to be excited about something
I really wanted to be in the moment with you
But my interests were split

We were almost at home
I hadn't looked at you once during our trip
The phone and computer had me transfixed
I did notice you were happy
So I could take this time to do my marketing
To write. To call. To post. To edit.
To do everything except tend to you.

Once we got settled in, I went right back to work.
Then, awhile later, I heard you talking
What were you talking about?
Who were you talking to?
Now I was listening.
Now I could hear you well.

You laughed and told someone about your day
I didn't know you had closed a client.
I didn't know it had taken you months to do so.
I had no idea what it all meant to you.
How had I missed all of this new info you're telling someone else right now?

I walked into the dining room
You were parked at the table laughing and chatting.
I was excited for you. I wanted to celebrate.

Finally, you hung up. I still don't know why I asked.
"Who was that, baby? And why am I just hearing all of this?"
You looked confused. Then hurt. Then accepting.
"That was Tina. I told you all this in the car after…"
You were still talking but I was stuck on Tina.

She was celebrating your good news a lot lately. She was around all the time, always smiling. Always looking fresh and ready, always tuned in to your needs, always calling at the wrong time. Now she was celebrating with you again. And where was I?

That night, I simply asked the question because I had to.
"How do you feel about Tina?"
You laid there quiet so long that I became unsure of if I had spoken to you. But I had asked.
You had heard me.

"Tina is just a good friend. She is always there for me. She's helping me build my dream and I trust her. You know, I love her, I guess. Not like you, baby. But you know…"

I laid there quietly pondering what you were saying.
"Why do you always go to her first when good things happen to you?"
Again, there was a long silence.
This silence held something. It was about to give birth.
"Actually, I come to you first. But you are always working. You are either writing a book, reading someone else's book, marketing books, researching grants, teaching a class or otherwise occupied with your coaching. I know how important it is for you to do what you do so I don't take it personal that you stopped listening to me a long time ago."

I could not deny that I had tuned you out
But my heart argued that I loved you and I was there.
What does there mean, though, if you aren't really there?

What was I doing but the same thing I had done before? This path is leading to loss.

I sat up in the bed and turned toward you.
Your eyes were as beautiful as they had been on the day I first loved you. Your energy was as warm and welcoming as it ever was. Nothing had really changed and I wasn't going to let it change.

"I'm sorry that I've left room for others to do what you want me to do. I'm sorry if you ever felt that my work was more important than you. I'm sorry that I stopped actively listening. I'm sorry for every night I made you come to bed alone and wake up alone, for every meal you wanted but I didn't make time to prepare for you. I'm sorry for every night you longed to make love to me but I chose to stay up and work, or was too tired to oblige you. I make no excuses. I love you now even more than I once did. Not one quiet moment was my heart contemplating about you because you are the one thing I'm sure of. I want to be what you need me to be. And when I am missing some cues, call me out on it so that I can fix it. I'm not willing to lose you, not your attention, not your energy, not your love."

We fixed it that night. We fix it every night. Because love needs maintenance and care. It cannot be put on autopilot.

Lacresha Hayes

Once

You were once just a photo.
A still shot, staring back at me from the other side of the screen.
You were once just an idea,
Flowing through my mind over and over again.
You were once perfect!

I was once curious.
I was once intrigued.
I was captivated with the thought of you.
I was content in your presence
Because to me, you were once perfect.

Now you make mistakes.
I notice imperfections.
We bicker.
I complain.
I yell.
You yell back.
But when I cry,
You console.

Now you forget important details,
I half listen to your stories.
You don't call when you say you will.
I don't answer when you finally do.
You don't compliment me every day.
When you do, I only half believe you.
You don't look at me as you once did,
And I no longer try.

But this morning, I looked at you.

Let Him Kiss Me

My heart was tugged,
And I fell in love all over again.
Now we have experiences between us.
Now we have damage against one another.
Now there stands an indictment.
Yet, in the face of all those tears I've shed,
And in light of all my own shortcomings...

I choose love!
I choose love!
I choose to go back to what was.
To make it even better.
To embrace you even tighter.
To love you better than I even once did.

Partnered

I know you're with me
And I am with you
I have your back
No matter what you do

I know you love me
You prove it every day
No need goes unmet
Even if you have to go out of your way

I know you trust me
To hold on to your heart
You placed it in my hands
From the very start

I know you watch me
I know you pray
I know you adore me
That's why I stay
Partnered

That Ahh!

I'm aching inside
I want you so bad
But you keep kissing
Licking
Lapping
Sucking
Touching
Hugging
Caressing
Romancing
Whispering sweet nothings
While my body goes wild
There's a throb between my thighs
A fire burning through my body
Passion ignited by the look in your eyes
The sound of your voice
The touch of your hands
The feel of your energy
I grab your face and bring it up
I rise up close
I smell your desire over your cologne
I whisper my longing
Plead for my need
And finally
FINALLY
You enter me slowly
Driving me mad
And I feel things I've never felt before
Before you
Before us
Before that amazing ahh!

Sonic Boom

I woke up before you this morning. I looked over at you, that beautiful skin with the hard muscle underneath, that handsome face with a youthful glow. I reached over and pulled the covers down to reveal all of you, taking in every inch and relishing the thought of what it feels like to have you inside me.

Just looking at you made my tummy tighten, my yoni ache with need and my mind twirl. Suddenly I wasn't sure what was going on but I felt an urgent need, a longing that shook me mentally, emotionally, and was nearly painful physically. I have never been the aggressor but I had to have you right then.

I crawled over on top of you and began touching all that skin, softly kissing all your favorite places, trying not to rush it while my sweetness throbbed with desire. You opened your eyes, staring eye to eye with me as I took you in my mouth. The look of ecstasy on your face energized my motion. My hands, my mouth, my moans all fell into a pattern with your breathing and thrusting.

The atmosphere was charged. The room temperature high. The sounds erupting from you created the climax-building mood music that led to repeated sonic booms being released between us. In my mouth, in my hand, in my yoni, in my booty, on my body, no area left untouched by the magnificent essence that escaped from you during our marathon of fun and freaky festivities.

Oh, the sure pleasure that rocked my core brought with it an answer to every boom from your body. Together, we created and destroyed universes until there was nothing left but the quiet calm of lovers spent, breathing in the aroma of truly mingled souls. You're spent. Energy drained. Motionless. You've given me everything and I've accepted it. Those powerful booms created a whole new entity called us.

Into The Deep

We were lying there breathing in the same oxygen, quietly enjoying the ambiance we'd created. You pulled me closer and held me tightly. At some point, I guess we both drifted off into a deep sleep.

In my dream, we were at a waterfall, naked and laughing, playing in the water, experiencing nature the way our ancestors once did. You were touching me all over as if you had 6 hands, no place unattended to. We were kissing and then suddenly there was no air, only water.

The Pisces in you encouraged me to go into the deep with you. You kept pulling me downward, beyond the place where the sun reached, where the water seemed dark, thick, weighted, full of a life and idea of its own. But I held on to you all while wondering how much deeper we'd go. I'd held on too long to let go, but my fear was beginning to show.

You continued soothing and consoling me, reminding me that no place upon this planet is adverse to the chosen. I was scared but yet I trusted you as you took me down beyond where any other life existed, assuring me that reward was on the other side of limits. I grew tired. I felt weighted. I felt lost. I felt unsure that we'd ever get back to where we began. About the time when I was getting reluctant to continue, there was a small flick of light in the depths. How odd!

We journeyed on toward the light. It grew in size and intensity. It was warm. It was inviting, as if it was there only for us. Suddenly the weight of the water disappeared. The colors changed from opaque darkness to a swirl of rainbow with a white light in the middle. The loneliness dissipated as suddenly once again there was life all around us. There was something beautiful on every side of us. I began to cry tears of overwhelming joy. But yet you didn't stop our forward progress toward that light that had seemed impossible to exist where it is.

Before long, we'd gotten so close that the light felt like intense white heat, like it should be strong enough to hurt or consume us, but yet it didn't hurt. You stopped and looked at me. You told me that most people spend their whole lives trying to get to the top but the truest treasure, the place where we come from, the source of our lives is in the deep. You grabbed my hand once more and we swam onward, slowly, deliberately. All the while, I kept looking at you in wonder. I could see you in a new and beautiful light. Your strength suddenly seemed overwhelming, but your tenderness even more tangible. I could feel your heart through your hand and I knew once again that I'd married the right man.

Suddenly, the light reached out and pulled us inside it, centered in the midst of an inferno of every color flame that seemed to give off no color at all. In that place, in the heart of this energy was wind that was both loud and quiet, forceful but calming. It seemed as if the light was permeating every cell, every fiber, every atom of me. I could feel pure energy pulsing through me. No voice spoke but suddenly it seemed as if the answers I'd sought all of my life were being revealed. No arms held me but I knew I was wrapped in the loving caress of my Creator. No air was in this place, but I was breathing better than I ever had. And across from me, looking me in my eyes, smiling and holding out a hand for me was you. You had taken me into the deep and we'd had an experience together that would never die or be explained away.

The tears fell and I wept with joy, with gratitude and with love. It felt as if ever tear I'd ever shed in life was released and I wept until I felt strong hands pull me out of that world and back into the present. I opened my eyes. It was still you, smiling at me as if you already knew my dream. We'd experienced beauty, truth, revelation, enlightenment, love together. We knew without saying a word. We'd gone into the deep.

Newness of Love

This newness of love
It's driving me to distraction
Everything you do
Feeds this burning attraction

In the morning
Before I can even open my eyes
I'm reaching for you
Making you rise

Before I can sleep
I need you inside
Whether you lay me down
Or let me ride

It hurts to deny myself
It's like I need you so badly
I know that I'm in love
But I also lust for you madly

Lacresha Hayes

Positively Yours

I'm positive it's you
With your radiant smile
Your amazing eyes
Your charming ways

You came swooping in
Knight in modern clothing
Positively honorable
Positively secure in who you are

Yes, I'm convinced it's you
Man of valor and dignity
Broad shoulders for the world
A backbone that's sturdy

I'm absolutely sure
That it's you I unmistakably love
And unapologetically adore
And that I'm positively yours

Let Him Kiss Me

Old Flame

My old flame flickered again today
He popped up in my inbox
I really didn't have much to say
But yet I felt the jolt

This morning you jumped out of bed
You didn't even look my way
Not even a kiss on the forehead
You were up and out the door

This afternoon you didn't answer my call
No reply to my text messages
You hadn't said a kind word to me at all
And I feel just a bit low

Then tonight you fell fast asleep
You didn't wait for me
My loneliness felt quite deep
So I got back online

And in my inbox is that flame
He's commented on all my pictures
He claims he still loves me the same
Looking at you asleep, I wonder if you do

I have a choice I have to make
I look at you and back at the screen
I choose the direction I will take
I close my computer and lie next to you

But even while lying there
I can't help but wonder

Lacresha Hayes

How much you would care
If you knew someone else did too

And if I chose this flame anew
He's a person, just a man
He may end up just like you
Taking me for granted

I turn over and close my eyes
The next time they open
I'm looking at sunrise
And your arms are around me

No old flame can compare
I snuggle in closer to you
You nuzzle into my hair
And I smile at a test I've passed

When Apart

Yesterday you had to hit the road
Which left upon my heart a heavy load
But I hid my tears behind a smile
Emotionally breaking into pieces all the while

I knew you were a king at first sight
I thought that I could handle this alright
Thought I could be strong for you
Thought I could do whatever I had to do

Yet watching you go, I felt like a child
Saying it hurt is putting it mild
Missing you makes my knees weak
Makes my eyes spring a leak

Now I lie here inhaling your smell
Wrapped in the t-shirt you wear so well
I remember why I fell in love with you
Because no one else can do the things you do

No one else can make the difference you make
No one else has the attributes it takes
A man who can touch my heart
Whether together or apart

Lacresha Hayes

This Morning, Trouble

This morning I awoke to hear you on the phone. The conversation was long, tense, and I could discern the stress in your voice. I wanted to rise up and run to your side but something kept me lying there in bed. I could tell you were pacing in the other room. I could tell you were worried. I could tell you felt cornered. I could tell she was a woman on the other end. And from the pain in my heart, I knew she wasn't just a fan or passerby.

This morning I awoke to new possibilities; those I didn't dare want to consider. When I consider how I fell asleep in your arms last night, I can't help but feel more than a little bereft. When I consider how much I think about you, how often I speak of you, how I pray for you, I can't help but feel cheated of something somehow to hear you say to someone else "I love you." But my ears did not deceive me.

Last night, you told me you loved me. You spoke about how much better your life is with me in it. You said you know God sent me to you. You kissed me and held me and called me wife. You talked of how you'd marry me all over again, how I was so perfect for you. But this morning I see that there must have been a moment when those things were not so because another woman is begging you to see her again, asking you why you remain here with me. I hear your explanations this morning and they sound weak even to me.

I sat up in the bed. I closed my eyes and said a prayer for us both. I could see before me two roads, but not clearly down either. I turned and placed my feet on the floor. I stood up and walked over to the door. I hesitated a moment. Did I want to stop the full marital assault in progress? Did I hope to save you? Save us? I didn't know what to do but my hand turned the knob and I opened the door. You turned and looked at me attempting to change the conversation. I shook my head as I walked up to you and reached for the phone. What was that expression on your face? A mixture of anger, fear and resolution?

I spoke softly into the phone and told her that you'll call her back with your answer soon and disconnected the call, all while looking you eye to eye. The questions flooded my mind then and the pain almost buckled my knees. Had I denied you some love, attention or adoration you needed? Or had I simply chosen the wrong man and put my hopes too high for you to fulfill them?

You spoke first saying that it was not as I think. Friendship gone one sided wrong, you said. But it was you who I'd heard say those three painful words. You did love her, you explained. But not enough to cheat on me or leave me. You expressed your side as I listened through the fog of my emotional pain. But I listened. I heard you say things that crushed something inside me... something... something... my pride. My ego.

You see, you're beautiful inside and out. I'm not the only one who sees that. Sometimes temptation gets so strong, you said, that you do find yourself entertaining conversations and late night phone calls while in your hotel room alone. All of these women look like models all day long, sending you pictures and videos all day long, begging, pleading and offering themselves to you everywhere you go. And then when you're home with me, there's nothing anymore. I'm writing. I'm working. I'm cleaning. I'm cooking. I'm tired. I'm sleeping.

You said I hadn't seduced you lately. No lingerie. None of the pretty pink lipstick that you like on me. Same hairstyle for months. You said you can't remember the last time you smelled my perfume. You said you can't remember the last time we did anything other than missionary. Oh, you had a laundry list of things you missed and I felt attacked. How fair was it that you could name all the things you missed without considering the other things you now had because of me?

You didn't give me credit for new deals I closed, the doubled income I'd earned, the possessions we'd accumulated together. You didn't give me credit for being there every time you called, for always having your back in business and at home. You didn't honor me for helping take care of your children by other women. You didn't even consider the weight of who I am and what I do. You didn't recognize how much I do and that I never complain. You only saw that the intimacy level had changed. I thought it was better because when you needed a shoulder to cry on, mine was always available and you never had to pretend with me. But you see it as worse because I'm too tired now to dress up in thongs and high heels, lipstick and a wig just to come to bed with you. You want me to remain forever sexy but I doubt you want it to hinder my productivity.

And for the first time, I almost hated you because you don't know how unfair it all is. You don't understand the pain of being a woman in love who tries her hardest just to have another woman who only looks good to come along and turn the head of the man you adore. You don't know the pain of sacrificing just to hear that it isn't enough, the inhuman expectations to be always beautiful, soft, wanting but also productive, dependable, contained, loyal and easy-going. You don't understand how it feels to look in the mirror and see gray hair knowing that someone 10 years your junior is sniffing behind your husband and he can't see past her perfect hair and hips.

You see, I don't look at the other men with perfect chests and feel temptation. I don't feel tempted because he smells divine. I see those who approach me with offers as trespassing upon divine property, as potential problems for the man I love. I don't entertain it, no matter how flattering they may be. How can I when you have totally consumed me? I am yours in every way and place that counts. To have that level of dedication and discover that you don't is crushing.

You grab my chin and turn my head up to you. I can't really stop the tears from falling because in my heart, I can feel the tear in a fabric that should never be compromised and I know we are at a crossroad. You speak words to console me, promising that you won't ever cheat, apologizing for letting your guard down, asking me to understand and forgive, assuring me that there is nothing with you and her, no love that I should be threatened by. But my soul feels what maybe you have not yet discovered. While I cannot explain it, the tears keep falling because I know it. I know it down deep. We are in trouble!

Lacresha Hayes

All I Can Be

I'm not perfect, fine by me
Still I'm trying to be all I can be

The cooking, the cleaning, don't mind at all
And still there to answer every call
But it does not matter how much I do
I cannot be all things to you

I cannot have "not a hair out of place"
Cannot always wear a smile on my face
Won't always be like peaches and cream
Won't always be the girl of a dream

Truly, I'm not perfect, which is fine by me
I'm just trying to be all I can be

Let Him Kiss Me

When I Prayed

When you love someone
If you've truly fallen in
You're not going to be still for the sin

So I called out to God
Father, please hear me
Don't let this rift be

Cover him, oh God
Keep his path free
Open his eyes that he may see

Also open my eyes
Penetrate my heart
Grant to us both a new start

Humble me, oh God
Purge me in every way
Help me trust you more today

Come in, Father
For he is only a man
Work in us both to accomplish your plan

Holy Creator of all
You have seen all my fears
You understand the reason behind all my tears

If there is any help
We know it must come from you
Show us what we must do

Lacresha Hayes

Bind us together
Sanctify us yet again
Don't let the enemy have my man

I bowed my head and said Amen!

Riptide

I woke up early this morning but I remained in place, lying there in thought. I looked to my left but you were not there. On the road again, doing your thing as always. Except, this time my trust is not there. I'm uncomfortable and worried, and even while I say that I'm not, I am.

I rise and pray. But even in my time with God, my heart is pulled and tugged and heavy. I can't stop wondering what you may be doing, who you may be with, and all the possibilities I once didn't consider a part of our lives. The tears begin falling all over again.

I labor in prayer for you before suddenly some small peace begins to rise up in the back of my troubled mind and grow. Along with it is a voice that whispers to me, "He is mine and I love him most. Will you trust me even in this?"

"Yes Lord, I will trust you. I can't help but trust you. Yes Lord, I trust you. Yes Lord, I trust YOU." I praise Him. I lift Him up. I keep praising and worshiping and saying I trust God.

After a few hours with God, I find the strength to get up and get on with my day. Client after client, I minister truth with grace and love, encourage the masses and even manage to get some decent writing done. As I was coming in for a nice deep breath, the phone rang. Odd number, but I answer just the same. Public figures and coaches can't very well not answer their phones, right? But of all regrets, I regret most taking that call.

"Hello."

"Hi. I know you don't know me, but your husband does." She rambled off her name, but really who wasn't able to hear at that point was me. I knew who she was. I felt this coming many mornings ago.

"Yes. How may I help you?"

"I don't think you'll do what helps me."

"And what would that be?"

"To walk away from the man I love, the one you married. You see, I know he loves me. He tells me all the time. But he feels he must honor his vows to you. I'm tired of seeing him torn, trying to have two families, trying to love two women. It's time something is done."

The earth shook under my feet, or maybe it was all in my chest. I know I was rocked! Devastation used to only be a word to me. Suddenly now, it was my reality. It was as if a riptide had grabbed me and took me out to sea. I was suffocating on emotions, choking on pain, drowning in heart ache.

"Family?" It was the only word I could manage. I wonder could she tell my heart was in my mouth and in pieces.

"Yes. I'm pregnant. He is the father and he knows it. It may not have been what either of us intended, but it has happened."

"Wow!" I thought I would have more words but there is nothing to be said. I'm in awe of the extent of damage one man can do.

"What are you going to do?"

"About what?"

"Everything I just told you."

"Does it matter to you what I do?"

"Yes, it does. My child will need her father."

Did this woman just say "her" as in she's far enough along to know the sex? Did she really say she's having your daughter? After all the trying and praying and begging God for another child, a girl, were you really about to have a daughter with someone else? How had I been betrayed by both you and God? Whatever strength that had kept me on my feet left me. I fell to the floor and I sat there. Suddenly, I knew exactly how Job felt on that day when his children were killed. He had lost it all. He was hurt. Hurt is common. Hurt can be managed. Hurt can be healed. No, he felt this,

THIS. He felt like a single drop of dust dropped in the middle of space, free falling and knowing that the bottom was a long way off and when he hit it, he'd die. He felt resolute to never be happy again, but mostly he felt betrayed by the only real help he'd ever known, by God.

"You're having a girl?"

"Yes. In 2 months. I'm tired of needing him and being told no because he's home with you, trying to hide me away. I'm tired of being relegated to second place."

She's crying now. She has the nerve to cry now. I listen and want to say a ton of mean things. I want to give her the business but then to top all betrayals, now my own heart betrays me because I feel something for her. Why do I feel for the woman who didn't feel for me when she was sleeping with my husband? Why am I moved to console her when she did this to herself? She knew he was married. She is not an innocent victim. She participated in her own heart ache while I didn't deserve mine. Still, I could not help myself.

"I'm sorry this happened to you. I hate that you have to go through this. I wouldn't wish it upon anyone."

She's all out bawling now and trying to talk and tell me her story through heaves. I listen through silent tears. I listen through my own pain. I keep listening. I keep consoling.

"I'm so glad you made this easy for me," she finally says. I laughed. I had to. God couldn't possibly love me. This had to be some form of punishment to have my world ripped apart and then to be the person who consoles the one who did it. I was angry with Him.

"I pray for you. Maybe God will work all of this out somehow. How, I don't know. But somehow." I was whispering. I wasn't sure I believed it but I said it, maybe out of habit or maybe a deeper self was speaking.

We got off the phone and for the first time in all the years of my salvation, I rued life. I hated living. I didn't want to go a step further in the land of the living dead. I wanted to go on to whatever is next. But I knew I wouldn't die because God is not that kind to me, apparently. I would keep living and have to find a way through this pain. Unfair. Unfair. Unfair was the cry of my mind while my heart continued shattering and the shattered pieces shattered more. Endless, bottomless, deep and dark ache. I was a goner.

Let Him Kiss Me

Baby Baby

She says she's having your baby, baby
Where does that leave us?
I guess that's a maybe

She says she's in love with you, baby
Where does that leave me?
In the land of maybe

She claims you as hers, my dear
But what am I now?
My place is no longer clear

I know I won't be here for another baby
It hurts too much
I'd go crazy

Even though I love you, my dear
You've found the one thing
That'll make me disappear

A baby for my baby
Inside I'm all achy
Hurting on the daily
A betrayed lady

Dear Diary

When was the last time I wrote in my journal? Almost 2 years ago, just about the time I got serious with this man. I guess I've been so busy with loving him that I'd forgotten about tending to me.

Today is a tough day, diary. I woke up suffocating on my heart which would not depart from my throat. He'll be home today, in fact any time now. I don't know what I will do or how to respond to all that has transpired. So many unanswered questions and the pain keeps coming in ever increasing waves.

Breathe.

Just breathe.

Remember to honor you.

God is real.

God is still on the throne.

God is sovereign. This is no surprise to Him. It may hurt but it is not going to hurt forever. Breathe.

I've showered and shaved and dolled myself up but my eyes are red-rimmed and puffy just the same. I went to the mirror and tried to smile earlier but it looked strained at best. There is no two-way street about it. My world feels flimsy as if I'm hanging on by a thread. How do I fix this? How does this all go away?

I hear his keys. God be with us both today!

Breaking Down

I see your face
I feel all the old familiar desire
I wish to replace
This burning fire

You kiss my cheek
I closed my eyes
My knees feel weak
I meet my demise

The tears overflow
I cannot keep my calm
Pressure begins to grow
Jesus, be my balm

You keep holding on
Whispering that you love me
Now my restraint is gone
You've practically destroyed me

I pull away from you
I cannot hide
It was the safest thing to do
With all the anger bubbling up inside

You cheated on me
You broke my heart
I want you to see
How you've ripped me apart

But as I continued to rant
Suddenly there was peace

Lacresha Hayes

I felt freedom and release

The breakdown had ended

Breaking Up

It's over! I didn't scream it but I meant it. I felt it inside me singing through my pores. He looked hurt.

"Are you hurt, baby? Did I disappoint you because I gave up?"

He asked me how could I give up so quickly. I asked him how he could devastate me so completely. The reasons he gave, the excuses that fell from his tongue seared my ears and my understanding.

He followed me upstairs as I began grabbing a few things to take with me. I'd been building a home here. It was too much to take with me. But I only need to remove myself. As long as I can hang on to me, I'll be okay. I will be okay. I keep repeating that like a mantra in my mind.

He blocked the door on my way out. He looked me in the eye and I saw tears form. I've been loving him so long now, running to his aid, that my heart nearly betrayed me. I very nearly reached out to console him. But this was no longer a relationship, no longer a sacred marriage. He was no longer the man I vowed to honor. He was not my partner. So I pushed past him and walked out the door without looking back.

Oh, if only my heart was so strong as to leave with me. No one ever told me that breaking up was not between two people but between one body. My mind in one place, my heart in another, and my body in motion but not truly with either my mind or my heart. Yes indeed, breaking up is hard to do!

Lacresha Hayes

The Fourth Rainy Day

It's been raining cats and dogs for days. I'm tired of it for many reasons, including the fact that we used to enjoy it so much.

I began working on a new book this morning, but even that has failed to keep me fully distracted. I miss my husband and that's all it is to that story. After weeks of being apart, I still sometimes wonder if I've made the right decision. Cheating sucks. It hurts so badly. But then so does leaving and dividing all we've built together.

The phone is ringing off the hook. I don't recognize the number so I've ignored the call twice. Now it is a different number calling. I'm so bored I decide to answer.

Within moments, my world is rocked! The person on the other end of the phone is a nurse telling me my husband has been admitted to the hospital after a severe auto accident. My space suddenly feels cramped. The air feels too heavy to breathe. And all that I can think about is how much I still love him.

I rush out of the house and head directly to the hospital. My hands are shaking and the tears are falling. I can't imagine losing him like this, while we're apart, while we're at odds with one another.

When I reach the hospital, I find the ICU. The nurse lets me see him. There are IVs and tubes and machines. His eyes are closed. His face is swollen and bruised. And my heart breaks into a million pieces. At that very moment, I realize how unimportant all of the past arguments have been. Regardless of what mistakes he's made; I've made them too. Can I judge his as worse than mine when I neglected him for so many weeks and months chasing the dollar, chasing accolades, following an image?

I walked over and grabbed his hand. I leaned my head

down to it. I whisper to God, or maybe him, or even myself. I was talking to us all:

I will never let you go again, no matter what mistakes you make, no matter how much it hurts to hold on.

How Faith

Dear Diary,

It has been three days and still he hasn't awakened. The doctors said that the swelling around his brain is decreasing but yet he hasn't moved an inch. I keep praying. I got him on every prayer list I can find. I have social media prayer requests circulating. Every pastor I know is praying. But nothing. I have faith. I know faith works. But how. How do I make it work for him?

I've begged God. I've pleaded. I've bargained. I've run out of ways to move Him, but if He doesn't save my husband, the doctors can't. How do you move the Master of the Universe to do a small miracle on behalf of two insignificant people who aren't great preachers or international prophets? How does faith work for the situation that everyone else says is dire?

Can I offer a life for a life? I'd gladly give mine to see him well again. What does God require of me to give me an audience with Him? How do I know what things He has ordained for this situation? Is my husband here because of some sin in his life or another? Is he here because of me and my anger toward him? Is he suffering behind those closed eyelids? Is he thinking of me? Or is he thinking of someone else? Have I driven him to this point where I don't know what's in his mind or heart anymore? Is all of this my fault?

The questions won't end. One brings another and another, but no answers. How, God, do I work my faith? How do I get through this? How do I believe you against all odds? I'm human and frail right now, afraid of losing the only man I don't want to live without. How does my faith apply now, when my whole life as I know it is on the line?

I only know that I must tap into my faith because losing my husband is not an option!

Twilight Miracles

My sister keeps calling
I finally answer the phone
She's been sick with worry
She doesn't want me to be alone

Against my wishes
She comes to my aid
My sister is like a savior
Her faith makes my doubts fade

She lifts me up
Makes me come out the low place
Reminds me ever so gently
That I must yet seek His face

She said to know God is to love Him
In that is everything
Because in that loving relationship
He'll show me what these things mean

She dragged me down to the chapel
At the altar we bowed our knees
Not sure how long we'd been there
But the Lord heard our pleas

The next thing I know
The nurse came in beaming
Maybe she was near tears
Her eyes were gleaming
"He's awake. He's awake."
I could hardly believe my ears
"He's asking for you."

Let Him Kiss Me

This brought me to tears

I turned to see my sister praising the Lord
"You've done it again, Master!"
You've saved us at twilight from disaster

Lacresha Hayes

A Long Trip Home

Dear Diary,

It's been a difficult few weeks. Truth is, it is a bit more difficult to forgive in actions than it is in words. As he heals up, I find myself revisiting my anger, not purposely. It keeps coming back to me that he broke our vows. Some days when I have to do extra things for him and I'm already busy and a little stressed, I actually snap at him and throw his mistake up in his face. I act pissy. I know he was wrong, but do I not have enough wrongs in this marriage to realize we must forgive?

Last week, he went back to work. My confidence went out the door behind him. He has to work with her. He is going to see her, talk to her. Maybe he's missed her. The thought brings a special pain to my soul. But then I am reminded of something my coach says all the time. This is nothing in light of the more important matters of life and the heart.

I have pictures of his vehicle after the accident. His vehicle was beat up more than he was. I made it my screensaver to remind me not to forget what I almost lost.

Last night, we finally made love again. It was like coming home. I was so skeptical. I wasn't sure I wanted to be touched by him, but I had to remember that is how we got into trouble the last time. I left so many opportunities to love him sweetly and passionately on the table. So I threw back a few drinks and I put on my game face. I closed my eyes and remembered where we began and went with it. Before I knew it, it was like nothing had changed, or maybe even had gotten better. The connection was back.

This trip home has been so troubled and still there is much work to do. But I try to focus only on what I can do within myself to help us forward. Home is worth building. Home is worth swallowing my pride. Home is worth being right and silent at the same time. Home is where my heart is and ultimately, I've discovered that he is my home. That, indeed, has taken a long process to learn.

Once Again

Because of you I have discovered
That yes, I can love again
Even after her, I'm your woman
You are my man

The key for me was forgiveness
Not as much for you as for me
I couldn't keep the pain
And still walk free

No matter what choice I made
I would have to release it either way
The process would hurt regardless
So I decided to stay

Even with your mistakes
I still look at you and see a king
I'm just as much in love
I would still accept your ring

I thought for sure we were done
Didn't think I'd love you once again
I didn't even want to try
But God had a different plan

Let Him Kiss Me

When I Shake

Dear Diary,

Today I had a very shaky day. Out of the blue, the memories of before hit me hard. I tried to call him but couldn't get through. My fears of these few peaceful months all tried to seize me at once. Tremors hit my heart and traveled all the way to my hands and then to my knees. I could barely stand.

I decided to kneel. Once again in all this peace my prayer life has gotten random at best. But it was God who brought us together, God who restored us after we split, and it has to be God to help us stay together in love, joy, peace and with honor and respect. As I found myself kneeling beside the bed though, a strange thing happened. I smiled.

I don't know how long it has been since my heart smiled, but in the moment that I decided to put God back in control of my life and marriage, in the center of all my fear, joy arrested me. And instead of pleading with God to keep my husband, I found myself praising God for my husband. I praised God for his life. I praised God for his heart, his purpose and his calling. I praised and I thanked and I poured my soul out in joyful gratitude. I was rejoicing so that I barely heard the phone.

Forgetting the shakiness of my pre-prayer state, I ran to the phone and it was my husband. He said, "Baby, you must be praying because I just felt a load fall off my shoulders unexplainably."

I told him about what had happened and he told me why I had been shaking. I was shaking because he was shaking. I was suddenly seized with fears from the past because he was suddenly faced with past pain and temptation. He said, "You may never know just how important it was for you to pray when you did, but I felt it. I felt new energy come over my tired body and mind. I felt clarity. And most of all, I felt you inside me. I had no choice but to honor what was real. You are real."

Today, diary, I discovered that my husband and I are bonded. Nothing is random. There is purpose in all things. I discovered a new connection. And I learned that when I shake to stand, that means I need to kneel.

Let Him Kiss Me

I turned over
You were wide awake
You kissed me good morning
Invited me to go to the lake

We sat on the pier
And you read to me
Song of Solomon
Now it made sense to me

Let him kiss me
I crave his mouth
The maiden was speaking
From the burn down south

Let him kiss me
The maiden's heart was aflame
She must have yearned for him
And now, I feel the same

Let him kiss me
Yes, she'd been caught
After all those lonely nights she found
The sweet love she'd sought

Lacresha Hayes

The Aftermath

Dear Sweetheart,

You know that these years have held many ups and downs. From the happenstance meeting to the amazing courtship that led to what we have now, I would not trade a bit of it. There has been mistakes and pain, some tears I never wanted to shed. But even those worked to build us in ways nothing else could have. We survived together.

People often speak about the power of love, but each morning when I wake up to you, I realize there is power in love. In fact, what we have, what we've been through, what we inspire in one another is proof that love is the ultimate power. Because of love, we survived separation, financial struggle, neglect, infidelity, sickness and outside influences. Love mended the cracks in our foundation. Love patched the leak in our roof. Love repaired every fracture in our oneness, and healed every place either of us hurt.

This morning I rose much earlier than usual. I had the blessed privilege to watch you sleep while listening to the sound of air moving in and out of your lungs, counting the rise and fall of your chest. I was lost in the thought of who you are and what we have. I didn't realize I was crying until tears dripped down on my hands. I smiled at them because I now clearly know the difference between tears of sorrow and these joyful, heart-happy, grateful to God tears. I now know the difference between the new, hoping for the world lusty love of the beginning of a relationship, and the tried, proven, fought each other, cried together, restored one another, forgave each other, love of a couple who made it through some trials. I thought I wanted that new, bubbly, skin tingling love of newbies until I tasted the deeper, more passionate, accepted and accepting of true person without masks love we have now.

There is nothing you can't say to me, nothing you can't do with me, no place we can't go together, no obstacle we can't overcome together. There are no secrets between us. We know the worst of each other and have already forgiven it. We encourage the best in one another. In truth, we've become each other, blended, our souls intermingled until there are no real distinctions. I love you and I love our journey.

You once asked me to open my mouth, to let you kiss me. And I did. I let you kiss me, every single piece of me, the physical and the metaphysical, has been kissed by you.

Sincerely,
Your Love

7 Days of Romantic Wonder

Day 1

When was the last time you decided that you were going to spend the day romancing your mate? This is the day.

Items Needed:
- Beautifully scented candles
- Bubble or milk bath
- Fresh linen lightly perfumed
- Sexy but comfortable lingerie
- Fruit platter or bowl
- Lightly scented or unscented massage oil
- Mood music

Depending upon preference, start the morning with breakfast that includes fresh fruit. Feed one another. Make sure you take a bath together, light the candles to set the mood. Give your mate a massage. Dance together or for one another. The biggest tip: TURN OFF THE PHONES! Do not do any social media. This day is all about you two and no one else. The world will not end without you in a day.

Day 2

Everyone has fantasies, even if not sexual. Sometimes, we are so busy thinking about how much we don't think we'll like something that we do not even try to hear and meet our partner at the point of their deepest desires.

On day 2, I want you to make a coupon for your mate granting them one sexual request of their choosing with no option to say no before you've tried it. The only acceptable exception is threesomes or anything involving other people. But between the two of you, take the boundaries off for a day.

Hint: being adventurous sometimes breaks monotony and helps create a closer bond, giving you two something else to remember fondly or laugh about together. So go on, climb a mountain and try to have sex while at the top.

Day 3

There is something about the unexpected sexual encounter. I can't tell you exactly how to do it, but I can give you a few ideas that you can tweak to meet your needs.

Try this:
- Pop up at their job and have impromptu sex, physical or oral
- Give them oral while stopped at a long traffic light
- Sex in the pool or whirlpool tub
- In the restroom in a restaurant (make sure it's clean)
- Movie theatre encounters are still fun

The point is not to plan it, but to let it happen on a day of closeness. Or to make it happen at a time when you know your mate is not expecting it. Trust me, they'll be thinking about it for many months to come.

Day 4

If you're a man, prepare her a foot bath and work her feet over while she watches her favorite shows or simply relaxes on the sofa.

If you're a woman, give him an unasked for back massage while he watches the news, football, ESPN or whatever he is doing to relax.

This day is about adding to each other's relaxation. To add fun to it, try to control yourself and not let it lead to sex. By the time you're ready for bed, you guys are going to be panting for one another. Can you contain it? Why try is the better question. Have fun!

Day 5

Time is a precious commodity. Today is about your time. Spend this day discussing the things you love about each other. No negativity. No buts. No ifs. Just I love you. I love this. I love that. This feels good. That feels amazing.

Touch each other. Make eye contact. Kiss a lot today. Say all the things you are afraid to say. Be vulnerable with each other. If tears come, let them. If they fall, let them. Go for a walk and actually hold hands, even if it feels odd at first. Grab her booty. Rub up against his chest and his penis. Make suggestive jokes and talk noise to each other. Tease and play. It's okay. All of that was made for you two. Have fun.

Day 6

Today is about remembering the beginning. Even if you don't want to, put something extra into your appearance. Send little sexy text messages to one another. Has he or she been asking for a dirty pic? This is the day to do it. Remember, this is not some random guy or girl. It's your spouse. But just because you're married does not mean you can't keep dating. Send the pic.

Whoever is first to get home, spread roses everywhere. Light some candles. Get some food together. Maybe even a protein or energy bar because you're going to need it for the night ahead.

As always, have fun!

Day 7

Today, I challenge you to take a ton of smiling happy selfies. Go to the photo booth in the mall and take some strips of pictures. Talk about what you've shared over the last few days. Today is the day of promises.

Tell her again all the reasons you married her and how happy you are with the last few days. Tell him what makes him a great husband and how you'd marry him all over again. Renew your vows again before God. Kneel and pray together and ask God to help you two make each other a priority as you have these past 6 days. Seal it with your own personal salt covenant where you two find a gorgeous container, crystal, and purchase two different brands of sea salt or some other salt, but of the same texture. Then pour all of your salt together into the container signifying no departure from this covenant until death or the salt can be divided exactly as it had been originally poured.

Then, make love. Make love as often as you can. Enjoy the sexual intimate aspects of your relationship. Do it so much that you begin to feel like you should be paid for it. Get tired of it and find a new way to enjoy it. Do it in every room of the house, except the kids room. Do it in the yard. Just do it. Stay sexually connected as well as spiritually and emotionally. As always, have fun and enjoy one another.

Let Him Kiss Me

Excerpts

Lacresha Hayes

KEEP TURNING FOR EXCITING EXCERPTS FROM LACRESHA HAYES

Earmageddon: Silencing the Earbenders

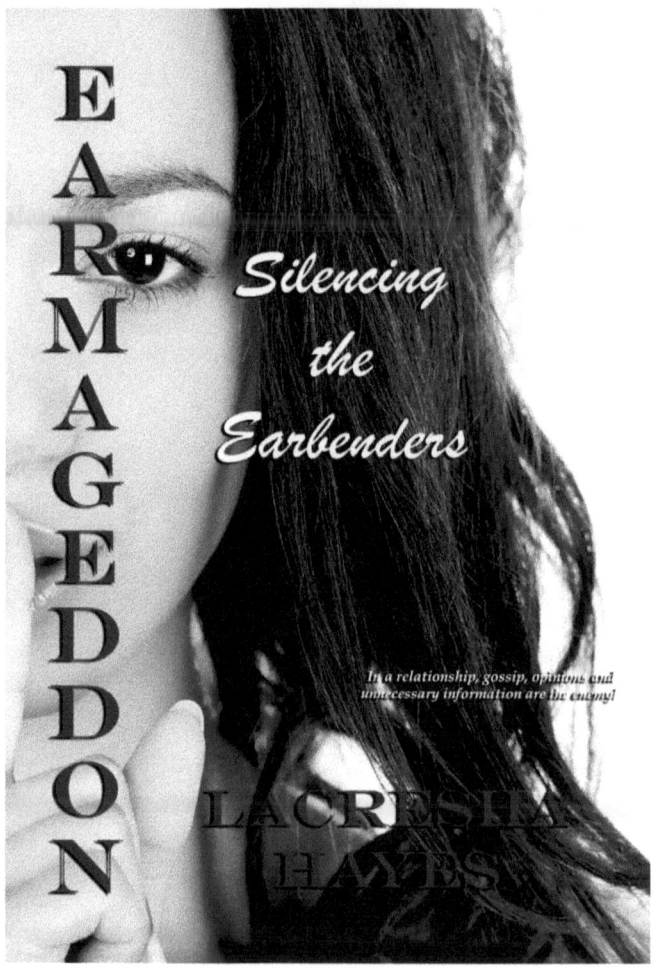

Chapter 1
The Thirsty Ear

My grandmother used to tell me, "When you go looking for it, you'll find it." I hated that saying. I'm still not crazy about it because in an ideal world, there would be nothing to find. But we aren't living in an ideal world, are we?

I was in a Skype session with a particularly accomplished client one day. We were supposed to be discussing the details of her beginning another business. But two minutes into the conversation, the session turned personal. She was apparently at a loss to explain why she was constantly assaulted with gossip about her chosen man. She just couldn't seem to get her family and friends out of her business. At the time, I didn't know the next question would become the premise of this book, didn't even have plans to do this book. But I asked her a simple question. "Why are you still listening?"

Verbal communication often require two things: a party to speak and a party to listen. As life goes, we cannot control the actions of others, including whether or not they will say something we may or may not want to hear, as the case may be. The only thing we have dominion over is our lives, including what we do, what we say and what we believe.

This is a very noisy world. There is and always has been something to listen to. But it is our responsibility to decide what we will listen to. Right now, there are people clamoring for you to believe like them in some area that your heart is already fix, but because you've decided, their opinions and information don't move you. You hear what they say, but you're not listening. It never touches your heart and barely even registers in your mind. That's because when your mind is made up, the thirst of your ear in that area is sated. But when your mind is searching for answers, your ears and eyes become thirsty for information that can help the mind decide. This is not a bad thing. It is how we grow, in so many ways, and shows a certain unity in the functionality of our bodies.

The ear thirsts for information to feed the mind to help it make solid decisions. Often times when it comes to relationships, we find that information ready and waiting for us, but it is not always the right information. Not every source is credible, but the ears do not possess the ability to discern credible information. This too is left to the mind, sometimes with some input from the heart. But until whatever issue the mind is turning has been resolved, the ears will be on alert for any information that relates to the issue. And thirsty ears wielded in ignorance will always lead to ruin.

Don't get me wrong, it is also the thirst of the ears that lead us to great discoveries. Thirsty ears are always listening to learn more so that the mind becomes more aware. It's a most joyous gift that God has given us, making it so that no amount of learning can ever dull the desire to learn more. May education always be a choice drug!

However, there are times when our environment is not conducive to listening. There are some things we don't really need to hear. And when it comes to relationships, we must truly use wisdom about listening. Having thirsty ears to know about your mate is dangerous when you allow others to tell you more about them than they can tell you about themselves. I'm not indicting the matter of truthfulness of outside information. Rather, I am making a case for the blank slate each relationship should begin on, something we'll discuss later. Suffice it to say, your love is going to make you hungry for more of your mate, but that hunger was created to keep two people fully engaged with one another, discovering each other like a new secret every day. It was not created to seek out those who are all too happy to bend your ear with both true and false statements about your mate. Just because it's true doesn't mean it is relevant. And every lie is a cancer waiting to destroy you.

KEEP TURNING FOR ANOTHER EXCITING EXCERPT
FROM

Adjacent Smiles: The Love We Make

Let Him Kiss Me

The Picturesque Scene

It's cold outside
And the trees are bare
The skies are dull
And as blank as a stare

But when you stepped out the door
I swear I saw the sun
Suddenly the middle of winter
Felt like spring had begun

Then you smiled at me
The temperature rose a few degrees
When you opened your mouth
Out came a summer breeze

I was taken right away
And there was no shame
Nothing to extinguish me
My heart was aflame

Where did this dashing prince come from when you weren't looking? Isn't it funny how love almost always blindsides you? I mean, you're sitting there swearing off dating, love and finally settling into your life as a single man or woman. You hadn't shaved in weeks. No special grooming. No attention-getting parfum or cologne. You are clearly not looking for love. And then, BAM, out of nowhere, it seems your heart gets snatched away!

Were you on errand to get a loaf of bread from the grocery store? Maybe you were in a long line at the post office or barbershop? Wherever you were when you were seized by love, it was a picturesque scene, not because of the actual location, but because of the miracle of connection. Let me tell you a little story.

I knew a young lady who grew up with pretty much the same white picket fence dreams as others in her generation. She always thought love would be tall, dark and handsome, chivalrous and brave. Though her life was tough, the little ember of hope that love would find her never died. It shifted in importance and thus as a source of major disappointment to minor irritation.

When she was young, she figured love would come early. As her twenties passed, she remained hopeful for her thirties. As they drew to a close, she had begun to think less and plan less to be a part of something special, of coupledom, but the hope still remained. And as spoken in 1 Corinthians, faith, hope and love abides. Her abiding hope was answered!

On a happenstance trip with a not-quite friend, she met the guy who would become her greatest love. You know, love is a funny thing and falling in love is as unique as the people who are falling. For some, it happens a lot like the movies, else the movies would probably not exist. For others, it happens in the strangest, most random of ways. For some, love happens in beautiful parks, scenic locations, mansions, premiers, and trips to exotic beaches. But in this instance, it happened in a trailer park. Oh wait! Don't laugh. Let me set the scene.

A dirt drive full of potholes. An old trailer. As she and her friend pulled up to the scene, she didn't expect to find love there. In fact, she wasn't even sure she'd find friendship or even mutual respect. She had no expectations. She simply hoped to find a few jokes and a good wi-fi signal as promised. But you gotta love the irony of finding what you are no longer seeking after wearing yourself out looking for it previously. I mean, how often have you torn the room apart looking for the remote, your keys or some other item that seems to have disappeared into thin air? If you're like me, you probably didn't find them in the heat of your seeking. It was after some kind of rest that what you wanted manifested itself again. Well, that was the case here.

He met them at the door, and I won't insult anyone by saying it wasn't love or even like at first sight. It was just a man who met two women at his door. He spoke and he joked and he interacted with his company, but there was no strikes of lightning or spiritual quickening. There was only the sound of a person being human. Still she had no clue that the voice she was hearing would become her favorite sound. She didn't know that the eyes she had only glimpsed would become her favorite pastime. There was nothing discernible in that first happenstance meeting. But he was paying closer attention than she was and the sun was about to break forth in her life! A miracle was brewing!

About The Author

Lacresha N. Hayes is the founder and owner of Lanico Enterprise and Your Healing Partner. She is head publisher at Lanico Media House and independent Executive Vice President with myEcon, Inc. She is also a trainer and speaker, as well as a social media guru.

Lacresha has written 34 books and counting with 20 titles currently on the market. She loves poetry and romance, but her writing generally possesses spiritual messages.

Lacresha works tirelessly as an advocate for healing from sexual abuse and domestic violence and is a strong proponent for traditional family life and general wholeness.

For more information, or to connect with Lacresha, you can visit her website at www.lacreshahayes.com or connect with her on Facebook at www.facebook.com/lacreshahayes

www.ingramcontent.com/pod-product-compliance
Lightning Source LLC
Chambersburg PA
CBHW070322100426
42743CB00011B/2521